W9-BKV-721

Pebble Plus

Exploremos la galaxia/Exploring the Galaxy

Marte/Mars

por/by Thomas K. Adamson

Traducción/Translation: Martín Luis Guzmán Ferrer, Ph.D.
Editor Consultor/Consulting Editor: Dra. Gail Saunders-Smith

James Gerard, Consultant
Aerospace Education Specialist, NASA
Kennedy Space Center, Florida

Capstone press

Mankato, Minnesota

Pebble Plus is published by Capstone Press
151 Good Counsel Drive, P.O. Box 669, Mankato, Minnesota 56002
http://www.capstone-press.com

1 2 3 4 5 6 11 10 09 08 07 06

Library of Congress Cataloging-in-Publication Data
Adamson, Thomas K.
    [Mars. Spanish & English]
    Marte = Mars / by Thomas K. Adamson.
    p. cm.—(Pebble plus: Exploremos la galaxia = Exploring the galaxy)
    English and Spanish.
    Includes index.
    ISBN-13: 978-0-7368-5880-9 (hardcover)
    ISBN-10: 0-7368-5880-6 (hardcover)
    1. Mars (Planet)—Juvenile literature. I. Title: Mars. II. Title
QB641.A3318 2005
523.43—dc22   2005019034

Summary: Simple text and photographs describe the planet Mars.

Editorial Credits
Mari C. Schuh, editor; Kia Adams, designer; Alta Schaffer, photo researcher; Eida del Risco, Spanish copy editor; Jenny Marks, bilingual editor

Photo Credits
Digital Vision, 5 (Venus), 19, 20–21
NASA, 4 (Pluto), 6–7, 8–9, 17; JPL, 5 (Jupiter), JPL/Caltech, 5 (Uranus), JPL/Malin Space Science Systems, 15
PhotoDisc Inc., cover, 4 (Neptune), 5 (Earth, Sun, Mars, Mercury, Saturn), 11 (both); PhotoDisc Imaging, 1; Stock Trek, 12–13

Note to Parents and Teachers

The Exploremos la galaxia/Exploring the Galaxy series supports national standards related to earth and space science. This book describes Mars in both English and Spanish. The photographs support early readers and language learners in understanding the text. Repetition of words and phrases helps early readers and language learners learn new words. This book also introduces early readers to subject-specific vocabulary words, which are defined in the Glossary section. Early readers may need assistance to read some words and to use the Table of Contents, Glossary, Internet Sites, and Index sections of the book.

Table of Contents

Tabla de contenidos

Mars

Mars is the fourth planet from the Sun. Mars is called the red planet.

Marte

Marte es el cuarto planeta a partir del Sol. Marte se conoce como el planeta rojo.

The Solar System/El sistema solar

Mars/Marte

Sun/El Sol

Surface of Mars

The red-brown surface of Mars is like a desert. Rocks cover the dry, dusty land on Mars.

La superficie de Marte

La superficie rojiza y marrón de Marte es como un desierto. Las rocas cubren la tierra árida y polvorienta de Marte.

7

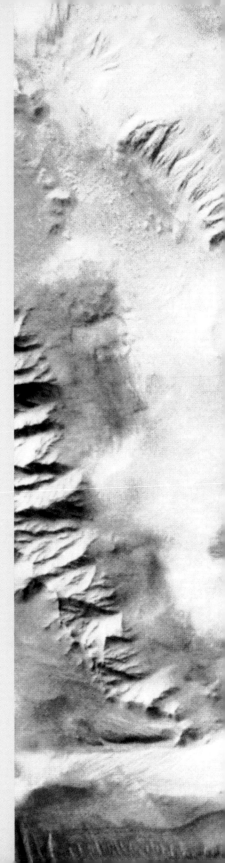

Mars has deep canyons
and huge volcanoes.
Mars has ice at its poles.

Marte tiene profundos cañones
y enormes volcanes.
Marte tiene hielo es sus polos.

9

Size of Mars

Mars is smaller than Earth.
Earth is about twice as wide
as Mars.

El tamaño de Marte

Marte es más pequeño que la Tierra.
La Tierra tiene el doble del ancho
de Marte.

Earth/La Tierra

Mars/Marte

Air and Weather

The air on Mars is thin
and cold. People could not
breathe the air.

Aire y clima

El aire de Marte es fino
y frío. La gente no podría
respirar el aire.

Dust storms happen often on Mars. They can cover the whole planet.

Las tormentas de polvo son frecuentes en Marte. Y pueden cubrir todo el planeta.

Exploring Mars

A trip to Mars from Earth
takes about six months. More
spacecraft have explored
Mars than any other planet.

Exploremos Marte

Un viaje de la Tierra a Marte
es como de seis meses. Sin
embargo, las naves espaciales
han explorado más a Marte que
a cualquier otro planeta.

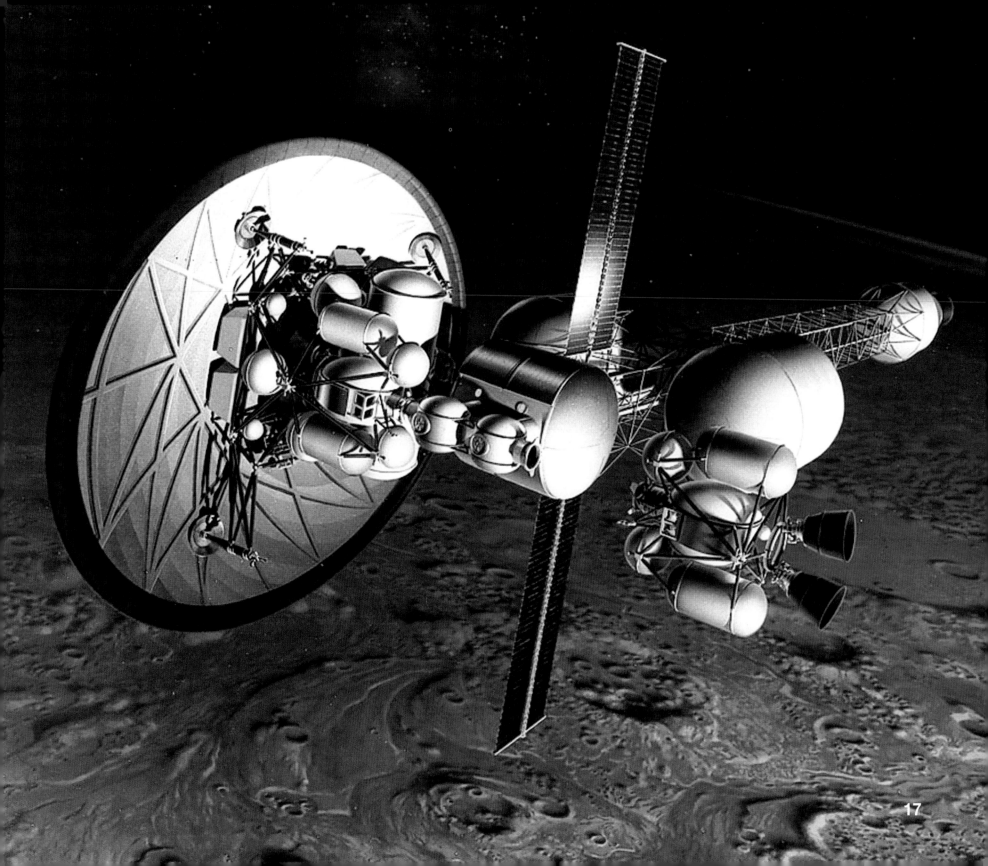

Scientists used a rover
to study rocks and dirt on
Mars. Scientists controlled
the rover from Earth.

Los científicos han usado aparatos
todoterreno para estudiar
las rocas y el lodo de Marte.
Los científicos controlan el
todoterreno desde la Tierra.

Someday people might live
on Mars. They would have to
wear space suits. They would
need to build shelters that
hold air they can breathe.

Algún día la gente podrá vivir en
Marte. Se tendría que usar trajes
espaciales. Y se tendrían que construir
refugios que conténgan el aire
que la gente necesita para respirar.

Glossary

canyon—a long, deep valley with steep sides

crater—a large bowl–shaped hole in the ground

desert—a very dry area of land; deserts are sandy and rocky.

planet—a large object that moves around the Sun; Mars is the fourth planet from the Sun.

pole—the top or bottom part of a planet

rover—a small vehicle that people can move by using remote control; a rover called Sojourner explored Mars.

spacecraft—a vehicle used to travel in space; spacecraft that have traveled to Mars have not included people.

Sun—the star that the planets move around; the Sun provides light and heat for the planets.

volcano—a mountain with vents; melted rock oozes out of the vents; volcanoes on Mars are no longer active.

Glosario

cañón—un valle largo y profundo con laderas de mucha pendiente

cráter—un hoyo en la tierra en forma de bol

desierto—un área de tierra muy árida; los desiertos son arenosos y rocosos.

nave espacial—vehículo que se usa para viajar en el espacio; las naves espaciales que han viajado a Marte no han incluido a personas.

planeta—un objeto grande que se mueve alrededor del Sol; Marte es el cuarto planeta a partir del Sol.

polo—la parte de arriba o de abajo de un planeta

Sol—la estrella alrededor de la cual se mueven los planetas; el Sol proporciona luz y calor a los planetas.

todoterreno—un vehículo pequeño que la gente puede mover con un control remoto; un todo terreno llamado Sojourner exploró Marte.

volcán—una montaña con respiraderos; por los respiraderos fluyen rocas derretidas; los volcanes de Marte ya no están activos.

Internet Sites

Do you want to find out more about Mars and the solar system? Let FactHound, our fact-finding hound dog, do the research for you.

Here's how:

1) Visit **www.facthound.com**

2) Type in the **Book ID** number: **0736821139**

3) Click on **FETCH IT.**

FactHound will fetch Internet sites picked by our editors just for you!

Sitios de Internet

¿Quieres saber más sobre Marte y el sistema solar? Deja que FactHound, nuestro perro sabueso, haga la investigación por ti.

Así:

1) Ve a **www.facthound.com**

2) Teclea el número ID del libro: **0736821139**

3) Clic en **FETCH IT.**

¡Facthound buscará en los sitios de Internet que han seleccionado nuestros editores sólo para ti!

Index

Índice